TALES OF DARK MATTER AND FIREFLIES

This book is for you, who wants to join our journey.

Bibliographic information from the German National Library: The German National Library lists this publication in the German National Bibliography; detailed bibliographical data can be found on the internet at dnb.dnb.de

First Edition published in Germany
Publisher:
BoD — Books on Demand, Norderstedt
ISBN 978-3-7526-4805-8

Ignatenko

I don't know what to tell you about.
death or love, or is it the same thing?

your love got called out
everything happened so fast
your eyes still half closed
the sky overcast.

shut all the windows! the power station's on fire.
I won't be long.

and while you were shouting
at that back that you knew
your heart already crying
I think it was shouting, too.

we were just married. we were together the whole
time.

you were up all night
waiting for his return
watched that distant red glow
watched your future burn.

I never saw the explosion itself. only the flames.

your love never returned, no
they just took him away
told you not to go near him
all thats left was to pray.

"they need to have at least 3 litres of milk",
my friend told me, but he doesn't drink milk.

you didn't leave him
you stayed by his side
bribed the doctors and nurses
took it all in stride.

*I'd have been with him 24 hours a day. I felt sorry
for every minute away from him.*

not one single tear left your eyes
not when his burns started showing
not when his body swelled up
not when you changed his bandages
and his skin pulled off with them
not when they told you
you'd chose that same fate
not when they put your love's body in a plastic bag
and another one
and a lead-lined casket
not when you gave birth to your
lovechild that died the next day

only when you realized:
your love will never call you again
in your dreams
you don't sleep
you don't sleep for the night skies,
they swallow your screams

*he spent 14 days in the clinic for
acute radiation sickness. it takes 14 days to die.
people don't want to hear about death. but I've
told you about love.
about how much I loved.*

Memoir of Ljudmila Ignatenko, wife of a
Chernobyl firefighter, published in "Chernobyl
Prayer" by Svetlana Alexievich, 2016.

while I'm stifled here
on the ground
in these jaw clenching thoughts of societies
necessities
my mind flies to where the stars breathe freedom.

you're fading, he said.
no, I'm transforming, she answered,
how can you not see the difference?

the universe oozes through every inch
of skin and sand.

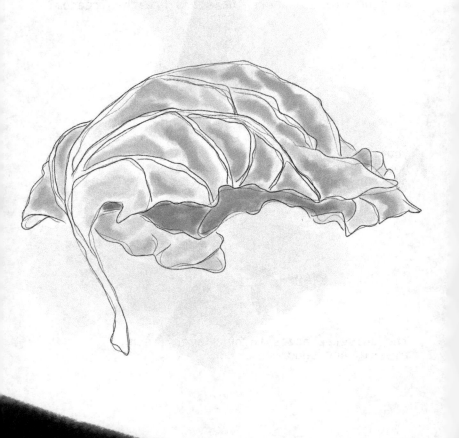

Monopod

your heart on your sleeve
and your soul in the air
your hope in the dead leaves
with all your despair

your toes in the ropes
and your spirit so high
your fingernails bloody
your heart in the sky

your hair in the wind
and your muscles — they hold?
your memories scattered
your message so bold

your ears hear them chanting
their voices so loud
while chainsaws are ranting
closing in on your crowd

your head on cold concrete
your hands holding bars
three months without sunlight
no birdsongs, just cars

you remember that feeling
50 feet in the air
your hope in the dead leaves
with all your despair.

I am water

for she is the ocean

the softness
that washes you clean

the force
that drags you under

the kindness
that nourishes you

the rhythm
that carries you to sleep

the weight
that crushes you

the love
that engulfs you

and the depth
that scares you.

why I am everything you
need.

facing reality

reality's breath down my neck
has always been heavier
than the thought of selling my body

you can numb your consciousness
to an extent
where you are more comfortable
in a room with a bull called lust
than in any social setting
where you are expected to represent
niceness and calm
the timid shy girl they see

however, the red light district
doesn't bear its name
from happy red lampions
and you know it!
how come this red glow is so comforting?

it's home and always has been

I've always known how to swing that red flag, my body
in front of the bull's eyes
play lust like Russian chess players play their
opponent
think-distract-check mate!

and oh, how they fell
one after another
into my lap and wept

it was the only time I knew what I was doing.

Why we feel so comfortable
being mere objects

hysteria isn't even cutting it

so this is what fucking 35 years
of growing up in western patriarchy
look like
and while I have no clue what took me so long to
get here
I certainly know it's not because,
but despite,
the fear, anxiety and general lostness instilled
into my head by society

so you think this is about me, when actually it's
not, but,
more about the girl on the street that barely got
herself to wearing a tank top today, cause, it's
too hot outside for a long sleeve

and the guy that catcalls her
from across the street
probably thinks he's going to make her week by
shouting
"what's up baby?"
and whistling at the bare skin he sees, but,
beneath that skin she's so paper thin, that, the
courage she still had
this morning is folding
while
memories like black hawks come down to get a better
look at their prey

chokehold. chokehold.
is all she can think as the air leaves her lungs
she wants to run but her feet won't budge then
he touches her
and she's back in that house her friends called
home
and she feels disgusted and so alone
and she's cold as ice but he won't let go 'cause
they never do

you might still think this is about me, when
it really is not

more about that colleague with the phd who's the
champion in her field
but she just can't see that

'cause when men feel threatened
they bark and bite
and they know how to get us, like, everytime
and the ones she looked up to, well,
she thought they were family
when in reality these alligators of academia spit
her out uncannily
with the biggest smiles
you'd have ever seen
on those sons of bitches

which brings me to my next question
I mean, honestly,
why is it always sons of bitches and daughters of
kings
for a king's daughter can never be a bitch, so,
where do all these bitches come from?

to be honest with you
I've never set eye on a bitch in my life and
neither tonight
all I see in this room is strength and pride and
love and might
and smiles and - oh believe me,
there are more balls in this room than in any frat
house!

just imagine what we could achieve together if we
stopped playing their games, so
unite and rise and remember
it was women who got these men on the moon and now
it's our time to space travel.

Why patriarchy is good to go.

while you were sleeping
we planned a revolution
while you dreamt a yesterday
we prepared for tomorrow
while you lost yourself in hate
we planted seeds of love
while you painted us naïve
we shared knowledge and tactics

while your head stuck in the sand
we combatted tides
while you were sleeping
we planned a revolution.

why we rise in climate science

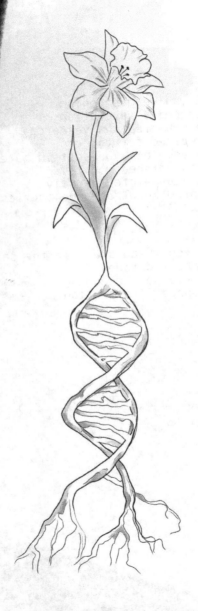

every touch of her skin, life threatening.

*Why some are not ready
for magic*

I have daffodils to smell
and dances to dance
I have bumblebees to pet
and fireflies to catch
I have 1038 tomato variations to taste
and some flirting to do
I guess all I'm saying is
I'm not ready.

*why cancer is a
fuckhead*

what's in this world but empty eyes
and borrowed identities.

Why that's not my
cup of tea

they say if you don't heal
what hurt you
you'll bleed on people
that didn't cut you
and I've tried
to brush off
the thousand cuts from hundreds of people
glistening on my aged skin
I scrubbed my surface
a million times
until that sweet red juice
your vampires love so much
kept showing repeatedly
but no scar
nor time
nor angel's juice
is ever able to the heal
the world's trauma embedded in my soul.

Why suffering is caring

in reality as in my dreams
jumping is no different
from falling
and neither is a choice.

Why it is all
downhill from here

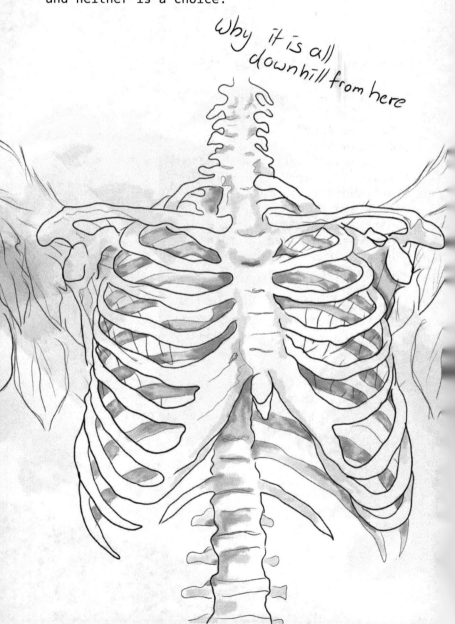

what if sitting
in this black hole
is as permanet
as death itself
what if the evolution of
feeling
is a lie
and these walls
lined with razor blades
are the only way
out of here?

if we can't see the stars
'cause our heads are too heavy
we'll find our magic on forest grounds.

when they say we're not like them
when they shut us out of
every social circle
that bears the "normal" label
when it rains too heavy on us
from every cloud they sent our way
we are still dancing my dear
we are still dancing!

Why straight
when you can be queer

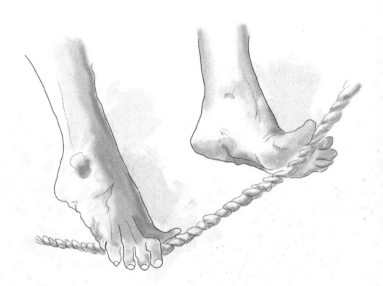

all I ever wanted was
to be seen
my art
myself
recognized
appreciated by the look in your eyes
little did I know you couldn't
appreciate art if it sucker-punched you
in the face
not even if it was wrapped around you
like my body
when I tried to make love
to your battered soul
oblivious to your inability
to love

as always, hopeful.

Why listening to your gut
is your safety net

Why are we addicted
to suppressants?

I believe it sad that today
we spend
more time touching things
than we do
touching each other.

everyone knows
the echo of the waves
but have you met anyone
anyone
who can describe
the echo of the clouds?

Why imagination beats
reality

maybe I'm too much
for you
but my gosh
wouldn't that be fun?

why I don't tell you

why I need you

and in your touch
a thousand light years

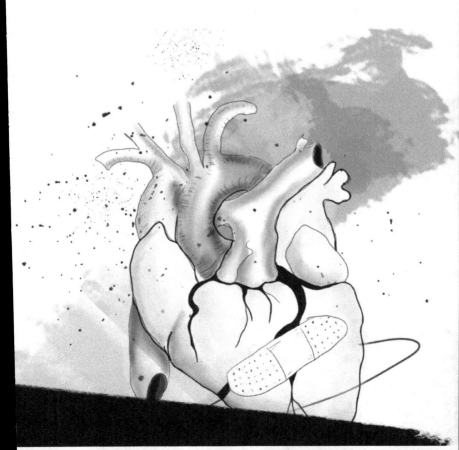

you asked me about my relationship
with the woods
as if it could be described
as if you'd never seen the fire
in my eyes
whenever my feet touch the forest floor
are you really not aware
of the forest's calmness?
the way my soul sings
with the critters and birds
and rests itself against the giants?
how I'm leaving a piece
of me
with every visit
because souls
unlike the rest of what makes us human
know where they belong.

why green
is the answer

your smile could melt
a thousand glaciers
I know
for I am one of them.

why a freezer would be handy
every time you step into the room.

be the person
that unhinges people
confuse them
with your taste.

why subtle isn't on the menu today

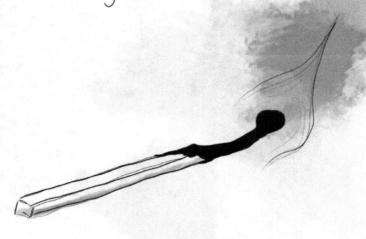

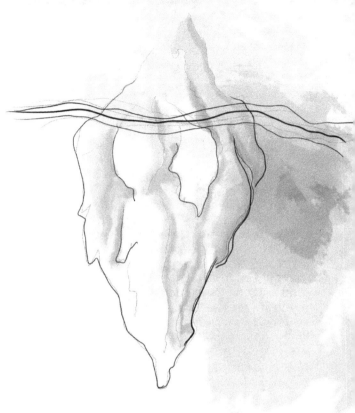

easy to please
and
easy to love
are two completely different concepts.

why you shouldn't
confuse me for the latter

true intentions

the consequence of betrayal
doesn't change its skin
just because you claim
the cause to be unintentional.
the Hurt drag the glass shards
of their shattered hearts
behind them everytime
they leave the house
no matter how much
you insist
you didn't mean to drop them.

she turned around
for the seventh time now
it was no use
"gone" she thought
that special glimpse of oneness
she tried to hold on to forever
that elastic band around her heart
this time it might have stretched too far.

I believe in silence

I'm not sure
what I saw
when I looked
into your eyes
you pulled me in
like gravity
like unwoven strings
surrounding me
dragging me
towards
your lips
are all I remember
soft cocoons
that together
with these black pools
that were your eyes
meant my downfall
in silence.

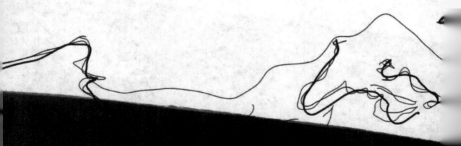

while she looked up
at the stars
the waves crashed
against her cheeks
violently
desperately
kissing her goodnight.

his rain was warm
and comforting
like winter nights
in Spanish taverns.

your empty bones
still weigh me down
all tears swallowed
by the earth
subscribed to you.

you treat us like an afterthought
like we could be replaced
like we would gracefully wait for your love next time
you'll turn around
be assured your eyes won't find the familiar
won't find a shore to hold onto
all the magic will be gone.

why you should pay
attention to a women
you love

trinity of falling in love

the beauty of falling in love
with someone's aura
is you're falling in love
with someone
unapologetically
all their has beens & magic
all their flaws and hopeful whispers.

the tragic of falling in love
with someone's aura
is you're falling in love
with someone
unknowingly
all their defense mechanisms & fears
all their life drafts so unlike your own.

the reality of falling in love
with someone's aura
is you're falling in love
for the tiniest present
and there's nothing
considered more lucky or doomed than this.

you were explaining one thing
or another
and I was only half listening
wondering how long
I had been staring at your mouth
if I was being too obvious?
but that mouth was smiling at me
seconds ago and I couldn't for one moment
not imagine the softness of these lips
brushing mine.

a girl can dream though

she beat him black'n'blue
and he was so grateful for a life in color.

summer madness

there was ease
sifting through your presence
as if a giant wrapped its hand around me and dipped
me into honey
your words were warm
your actions sincere
as I opened my heart

to let your love
flow through my veins
engage my bones in an everlasting dance

you left.

how many pictures do I need to take
to forget that I'm forgetting to forget
you
and can anyone grasp
that the word for-get
is full of the most selfish thing
called longing
for something, someone
always someone
always time with someone
always thoughts of that time with someone
I tend to forget a lot these days.

but never you

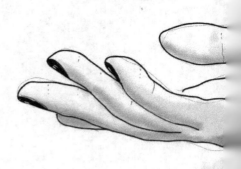

release me

you are so beautiful
the most beautiful soul
I've ever known
you shouldn't be the last page for anyone

you should be the climax
the build up
the growing intimacy
the endless moonlit nights
and careless days at the beach
the fluttery chaos of butterfly chatter
a happy ending everlasting.

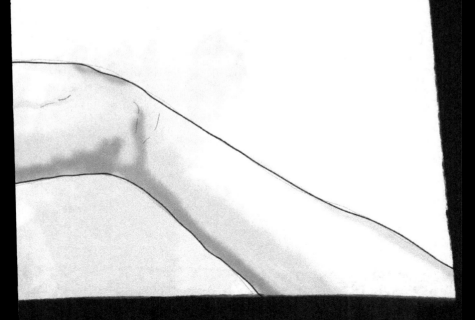

would you follow me into the woods
if I promised you magic?
would you follow me into the waters
if I promised you a billion lights?
would you follow me?
would you follow me?

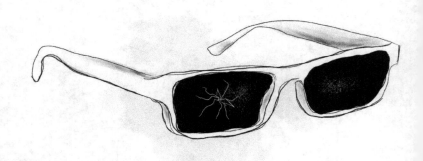

why white was always innocence
and black was always sin
he never quite understood
wasn't it black nights that gave comfort
while a white out scared people to death?

hope is always
the last
to leave the room
she closes the door
quietly.

he might just as well
have been a thought
inspired by a past life.

she saved so many people
she completely forgot about herself.

it is written
nothing is permanent
and that's were all our hope lies.

maybe it's not about trust at all
maybe it's about not being so afraid all the
time.

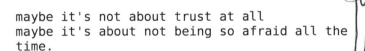

the trial

people say you shouldn't have any expectation ever
to not be dis-appointed
and I ask myself if in return it means
to never be appointed to anything
maybe not to that stone cold lump of sadness
curling up in my stomach like that
sorry excuse for a cat from next door
on my door step
expecting me to let her inside
to sharpen her claws on my night stand
whilst half daring me to not open that door
squinting at me with her glowing devil's eyes
so she can get back at me
when I least expect it

so if in conclusion
no expectation means no percevearance
means no motivation
means no will to get up in the morning
means standing still
then I would rather be appointed
to this sadness
or whatever feeling is coming down to me
from the night sky I lose myself in
the darkness I'm searching for to match my sadness
a blanket of dark matter to cover my tears
cover the disappointment

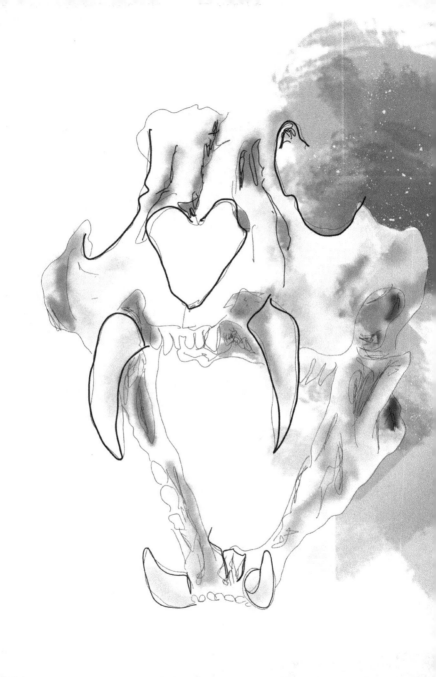

just like a king he stood and swayed
whispering stories into ears
so eager to listen
while hearts were torn and souls sank
into the flooded sands of time

Why trees are
better teachers

that kitted cupboard

if there were a quote
for this feeling
it would be something between
concrete and hurt
and flowers and love
and brick and despair
and canvas and tears
and open hearts and your face
definitely your face

sometimes the most unlikely edges
shine as bright as the sun
on a clear day.

sometimes…
the waters closest to the shore are the calmest.

the flowers planted in her garden
had nothing on
the flowers growing inside her soul.

however lost he felt
he knew
he could always be found
between the moon and her shades.

thorns don't grow easy
nor are they easily removed.

a heart on fire

he said
you shouldn't throw your heart
at everyone so quickly
I said
it's a present
no one is willing to hold onto
for too long anyway.

chaos

whenever I listen to all these astrophysicists
say that ultimately
all of the universe is chaos
and only us humans strive for something more
orderly
I wonder if I'm actually in line
with the universe
when I'm all over the place again & again.

and isn't it kinda normal
that I'm drawn to you
whose body has chaos written all over it
who runs through my head
like a tornado on speed
wrecking every single molecule
in its path.

so chaos?
maybe I welcome you too openly
or maybe you are the manifestation
of universal matter
whose eyes confuse me by spelling
chaos backwards
replacing every single letter.

let's dive around the moon,
embrace collapsing stars.

do you believe that
if we leaned against the wind
our hearts would beat again?

words are only the hollow halls
of deeds undone.

there won't be any truths told
during a storm of words

contents are hot pt1

this is how love should be
consumed
he thought
slowly whilst hot
however, this was rarely
how it played out in life
love, it seemed
does not like to be stretched
held back
instead it rolls over you
like a tidal wave
drags you into the depths
of desires' ocean
plays with you
wrecks your brain
until
well, until it spits you out
washes you ashore
and there you lay

exhausted.

contents are hot pt2

that's what reading Russian
literature did to him
he was more aware
of the moment
his duty
and his duty at the moment
was to serve
making these people
feel seen
feel appreciated
will it make them feel so good
they will return
more easily?
will it fill their empty souls
enough to last
through the week
keeping them away
from
these deadly machines?
he sipped his coffee
slowly
for it was still hot.

may I ask you
to step aside, please?
take your beauty outside
for awhile
air out that twitching eye from when
you lied
to me again
there's nothing much left here
for you anyway.

honesty.

I still think of you
sometimes
like my shoe gets caught
in that exact same crack
in the street
makes me stumble, examine it
for awhile
stroke it, smile

I still think of you
sometimes
and I really don't know
what happened
to our story or if it's important
isn't it strange though
that I'm still learning a language
just because you said
I couldn't do it
too complicated
(maybe these are the words to describe
our friendship)
but I wouldn't give
that up, that's not
who I am
I keep telling myself
maybe it's a language
my grandma spoke once
I never asked her

I still think of you some
time's a peculiar thing
leaving traces of itself
all over the place
(maybe these are the words to describe me)

there are pieces of
my pain
in some Lithuanian crime series
pieces of our story
in some human archive or other
like my poems, your pictures
and these memories
of someone who
saved me
once

I still think of you
sometimes
this guy who talked me
off that bridge
with Nietzsche quotes
while the demons I faced were
too much
like his own
insecure, stubborn
(these words most definitely describe you)
with the biggest heart
so little of us have
to deal with

I still think of you
sometimes
I wish you well.

Sylvia Gassner

The author, born and raised in the depths of
Bavaria, discovered her artistic talent, even
though some (especially her parents) wouldn't
suggest singing at 6.00 am in the bathroom counts
as such. Ever since she was lead by life choices
who brought her vulnerably back to an urge of
releasing the world's pain buried inside her heart
through photography and poetry. "Tales of Dark
Matter and Fireflies" is her first poetry selection.

Sylvia would like to thank especially her friend
Ella for stepping on her toes time and time again
to present her art to a wider audience. Furthermore
she would like to say thank you to her family and
friends, most of all her partner Matze for being
the person to love her the way she deserves to be
loved. Finally she would like to thank you, the
reader, for supporting her art.

Sara-Lena Moellenkamp

Born and raised 1987 on a dying planet called earth
and after working as an assistant director and in
a marketing job, Sara-Lena decided to look for the
beautiful in the gloomy and the gloomy in the
beautiful. She remembered that she once studied
literary, arts and media studies and loves
drawing. So she took this toolkit to explore the
freedom of visualizing imagination. "Tales of Dark
Matter and Fireflies" is her first book.

Sara-Lena would like to thank her family for
supporting her unconditionally in all situations
that crossed her path. And she would like to thank
her soulmate Felix and all the friends and gorgeous
people who are or were part of her life so far.

CPSIA information can be obtained
at www.ICGtesting.com
Printed in the USA
LVHW081441241120
672563LV00003B/186

CPSIA information can be obtained
at www.ICGtesting.com
Printed in the USA
LVHW081441241120
672563LV00003B/186

9 783752 648058